Google SEO for Bloggers

A Step-by-Step Strategy for Getting Google Love

The Step-by-Step Process I used to Rank More than 1,700 Keywords on the First Page of Google

Want to know the secret to being successful as a blogger or in any business? Find out the part of the business that other entrepreneurs avoid and become a Rockstar to jump ahead of the competition.

Asking my blogging colleagues about their strategies to rank on Google, I was amazed to hear from nearly everyone that they really hadn't paid much attention to search engine optimization (SEO).

Despite the fact that most depend on Google for 60% or more of their blog traffic.

It's the kind of aha! moment you get that rockets your business into the stratosphere!

How I put together a Google SEO process to more than double my search traffic

I determined to learn everything I could about Google SEO and getting on the first page of the world's largest search engine.

I put together a process for every post I wrote and the results were astounding.

I almost tripled my Google search traffic over the next year and have doubled my monthly income.

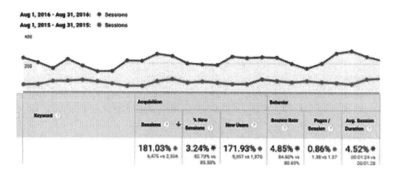

Best yet, using it frequently means I've perfected the process and now it takes very little time to rank a post on Google.

8 Steps for Eye-Popping Search Traffic with Every Post

Don't fool yourself. You aren't going to rank on Google with just any disorganized collection of SEO tricks. The top spot in search gets nearly a third of the clicks and competition is intense.

Getting to #1 and staying there means you'll need to implement a complete process of on-page and off-page SEO that blows everyone else away!

I'm sharing my entire process to rank posts on Google, from how to find the keywords you can actually rank to the secret that triples my traffic and makes more money on each post.

If you are serious about boosting your blog traffic, I mean really serious about learning how to make a blog rock and ready to do what other bloggers avoid, then don't miss your chance at this Google SEO process.

It's time to get the Google love you deserve. Let's Do This!

In this book you'll learn:

- Why most bloggers don't make money on search traffic and how to get the right visitors. (pg. 7)

- 126 easy links you can get that boost traffic and search rankings. (pg. 46)

- How to tell if you can rank on Google's first page before you waste your time. (pg. 10)

- The one SEO step that nearly triples my traffic. (pg. 77)

- What to do once you reach the first page of Google and how to stay there! (pg. 84)

My Work from Home Money is your source for work at home ideas and strategies. Financial freedom isn't about having lots of money, it's about making money doing the things you enjoy...and that's exactly what this blog will help you do.

I've spent years working freelance, blogging and searching for different ways to make money. I've made more than my share of mistakes and seen more scams than I can count. I've also created my dream job and make more than I ever did in the rat-race.

This isn't about not working. I don't promise you a 4-Hour Work Week. What I do promise is that you'll find something you enjoy doing, that you'll find the way to make money doing it, and that you will be in control of your own financial future for the first time in your life.

Joseph Hogue, CFA

Born and raised in Iowa, I graduated from Iowa State University after serving in the Marine Corps. I worked in corporate finance and real estate before starting a career in investment analysis.

Working in the corporate world, I realized there was something missing in the 9-to-5 rat race. I was making lots of money but hated my job and realized...who wants to be rich when they're old if they spent a third of their life miserable.

I now run six websites and love my work-at-home life. How much I make and my work life is completely up to me. I no longer worry about saving for retirement because I can't imagine ever doing anything else.

ISBN 978-0-9971112-6-2 (digital)

ISBN 978-0-9971112-7-9 (paperback)

Contents

Google SEO Decoded:
How to Get that #1 Spot

Writing to rank on Google is something a lot of bloggers just don't even think about. Visit one of the many websites dedicated to Google SEO and you hear that writing quality content is all you need to get a first-page spot on the search engine.

It's an easy answer for bloggers but is also completely, absolutely wrong!

If just writing quality blog posts was all it took, then 95% of bloggers wouldn't be quitting within the first six months of launching their websites. These are legit bloggers with something to say and getting no love from the world's largest search engine.

Why? Because it takes a lot more to get your blog ranked on Google than just putting words on the virtual page.

The good news is that putting together a Google SEO strategy will put you ahead of the vast majority of bloggers and will boost your traffic through the stratosphere.

Why Google SEO Matters

According to WordPress, bloggers create more than two million new posts every day. Most of these posts are just updates or ramblings with little hope of making it anywhere on Google.

But should that matter? Why not just focus on the interaction with your readers with new content?

How about another question, does it matter how great your blog is if nobody reads it?

Traffic from Google search accounts for between 55% and 80% of most blogs' total traffic. Search traffic averages 68% of my 50,000+ monthly visitors across six blogs. That's more than 35,000 monthly visitors thanks to ranking on the first pages of Google, free traffic that I wouldn't have otherwise.

You'll see some search traffic by just creating content for your blog but it's not enough. Getting real Google love means getting to that first page.

Anything after the first page is just wasted words.

A study by Chitika shows that the first ten search results on Google get almost all of the clicks from searches with the top five results getting 75% of clicks.

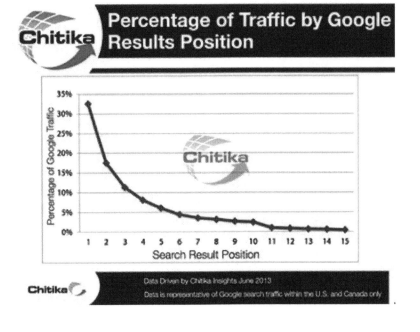

Now that Google has moved all the ads to the top of search results, regular blog posts may be getting much less of the total traffic. In another survey, most internet users were unable to tell the difference between ads and organic search results.

That means those two or three ads at the top of a Google search are getting the majority of clicks and makes a great ranking strategy even more important for bloggers.

Hiring a SEO company to help you rank will cost thousands a month, minimum. Avoiding a good SEO strategy will cost you thousands a month in lost sales.

There is a DIY solution!

Turns out, ranking on Google isn't that tough if you put in the time to learn what it takes to boost your posts to the first page. I rank for 1,728 different search terms on the first page of Google and that's just the first page!

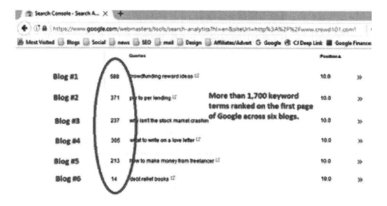

The secret is a Google SEO strategy, a process you use with all your posts that is quick enough to not take all your time but effective enough to get results.

What Kind of Articles Make it to #1?

Google ranks pages…not blogs. Do a search and almost all the results will be individual pages on a website rather than the home page.

It may seem a trivial difference but it hugely affects your Google SEO strategy. Most bloggers work on getting their home page ranked, building the SEO value of their whole site, when they should be trying to rank each individual blog post.

Google is usually extremely tight-lipped about how it ranks websites. In a break to this secrecy, Google's Andrey Lipattsev said in 2016 that the two most important factors are content and links.

Let's look at content first.

Writing the kind of posts that Google loves goes a lot further than just writing interesting content.

Using keywords with just the right level of competition and traffic

Understanding how to show Google what keywords are important in your post

Making your posts interesting through tables, images and other media

Tricking out your post to hit Google's checklist for reader experience

Writing content that gets ranked in search goes beyond posting each week to your blog and learning how to write for search is just as important as writing for your readers. We'll cover all of these and more in chapters dedicated to putting your content on SEO steroids.

As for links…

I was surprised how little most bloggers know about link-building when I first started paying attention to Google SEO. I reached out to a group of financial bloggers I knew, a group that had been extremely helpful in getting started blogging.

I asked what link-building strategies they were using and if they had any advice…

The overwhelming answer was, "I haven't done any link-building strategies."

These aren't the average blogger that updates their site every couple of months and never really makes any money. A lot of these bloggers get tens of thousands of visitors each month and make thousands on their websites.

But they've never paid much attention to a real SEO strategy. They get good traffic just by virtue of having hundreds of posts on their blog and being around for a few years…but are missing out on the real potential for search traffic.

Link-building is about making it easy for Google and readers to find your articles, and about showing the search engine which posts are important for which keywords.

- Building links on your own website to highlight information and keep readers on your blog

- Using SEO strategies like the Hub-and-Spoke to create a complete reader experience

- Getting links from guest posting and other strategies to increase an article's ranking

How this Book will Help You Rank on Google

Getting ranked on Google is an afterthought for most bloggers. They spend hours, sometimes days writing a blog post and then hope it goes viral and attracts the kind of attention they need to show up in search.

That's fine if you just want a hobby-blog. If you just enjoy writing and don't care about increasing blog traffic or making money on your site…just keep doing that.

If you want to get each post to rank in search and if you want to make as much money as possible blogging, you need a Google SEO strategy you can use with each post.

That's what this book is all about.

The nine chapters lay out a complete SEO process for planning, writing and ranking each blog post. Being able to put everything in a process will help use your time most effectively without getting lost in all the parts of a successful SEO strategy.

Not only will you be able to use this Google SEO process for ranking new blog posts but also to improve the rankings on existing posts. In fact, the final chapter shares a strategy I use to boost existing posts. It's a strategy that has nearly tripled the traffic to each post and almost nobody is using it.

Ranking your blog posts on Google doesn't have to cost thousands in SEO services. Putting together a Google SEO process is all about understanding what works in search engine optimization and how to make it natural to your blogging process.

Keyword Research:
Ranking for Readers Ready to Buy

What if you could boost your blog traffic by hundreds of visitors for every post you wrote?

Would it be worth an extra 15 minutes per article?

Writing six posts a month, that means an extra 20,000+ visitors in your first year of blogging.

Keyword research can be a pain and most bloggers avoid it altogether. It's one of the biggest mistakes in blogging and even those checking the basic boxes for keyword ranking may not realize just how important it is.

In fact, you could be wasting your time if you're not using a simple process of finding the keywords that will bring targeted traffic to your blog.

Case in point, I got lazy with keyword research on one post that I was sure was going to make me loads of money. I used my entire SEO strategy on the post from basic on-page SEO to boosting links with pdf and audio and I even wrote eight guest post for other blogs and linked back to it.

This should have led to a surge in the Google ranking for the post and the potential to make some great money on affiliate offers.

The result. Next to nothing. I make a little on the post but not nearly as much as I should have because I missed two very important problems that keyword research fixes – competition and buyer intent.

They are two of the most basic problems in Google ranking and making money and its where you need to start your SEO process to be successful.

We'll start off with some of the basics before we get into my complete keyword research process that will not only help you get that #1 rank on Google search but will attract the right kind of readers that will make you money!

What is Keyword Research?

The way your blog shows up in Google search is by ranking for keywords which can be one word or a string of several words. For example, 'money' is a keyword while so is 'make money blogging from home'.

The entire idea of search engine optimization (SEO) is to make it so you rank more highly for keywords than other pages on the internet.

Keyword research is the process of finding the keywords that you want to rank for on Google, which ones will bring you the most visitors and which ones will make you the most money.

It's a simple idea that can mean the difference between building a profitable blog and just wasting your time even on the most well-written posts.

Why is Keyword Research so Important for Bloggers?

Google search traffic accounts for between half and 80% of total visitors for most blogs so if you are not ranking for keywords then you are only scratching the surface of what's possible with your blog.

You might be saying, "I get traffic from Google and don't do keyword research." Just about any blog will get some traffic just by having a lot of articles but it's nothing compared to what you could be getting.

Look at the Google Webmaster Search Analytics for my post on making money on Craigslist. The post gets nearly 800 clicks a month from almost 1,000 Google search terms. Some of the keyword phrases rank really well, many on the first page, but none of them are ranking in that top spot.

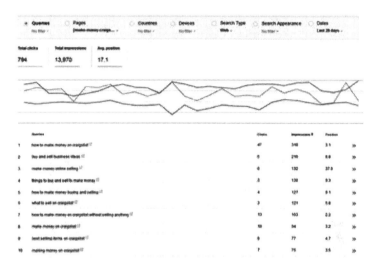

Since the top two spots in Google search results get up to half the clicks, I'm missing out on a lot of traffic by not ranking the post higher.

Even the bloggers that actually take the time to do keyword research for a post will often stop at simply finding popular keywords with a high volume of monthly searches. The problem is that good keyword research means finding the terms with good volume AND that you can rank for on Google.

Try writing a post for just any high-volume keyword and all you'll hear are the crickets chirping.

Look at this screenshot of the Google results for 'Make Money'.

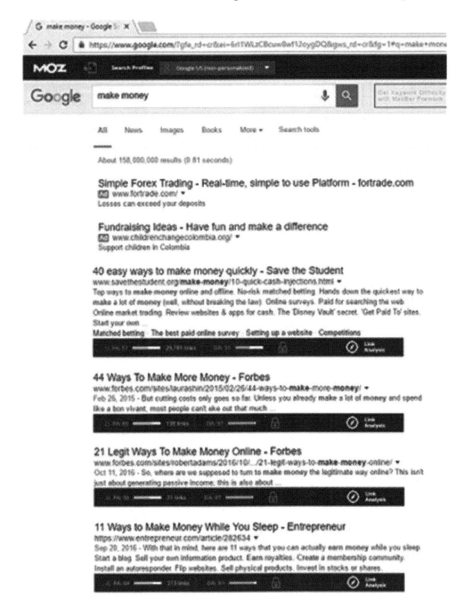

Now this keyword gets nearly 100,000 searches a month, why wouldn't you want to optimize an article around the term?

Because you'll be lucky to make it to page five on the search engines.

First, you've got to contend with Google Ads at the top of the page. Businesses target these top keywords and take a big portion of the clicks when someone searches for anything that can make them money.

But look at the websites that are in the first four spots in the search. Do you think your blog is going to outrank Forbes and Entrepreneur? I cut off the page but the bad news extends all the way down through the 1st page of Google with mega-websites like LifeHack and The Penny Hoarder.

You'll notice that my search results with the little black bar may look a little different than what you see. I installed a free keyword research tool called MozBar that will make a huge difference in your keyword SEO and something we'll hit on later in this chapter.

So understanding the competition for getting your post on the first page of Google for a keyword is critical but it's not the only reason why keyword research is so important.

Remember that post that I spent so much time on but didn't make any money? It wasn't because it wasn't getting any traffic. I built the article up to over 5,000 page views a month and was getting over 1,000 clicks through to the affiliates on the page…but few of them were buying!

It's called the buying process and the visitors I was getting just weren't ready to buy anything yet.

Let's first look at understanding which visitors you want to attract to your blog, the ones that will make you money, and then we'll continue with my complete keyword research process.

Buyer Intent and Keyword Research:
Getting the Clicks that Matter

All purchases go through a buying process before a decision is made.

1. The person becomes **aware** of a problem or about a product

2. Information helps answer questions the buyer has about the problem and products, building **interest** in potential solutions

3. The person finishes their search for information to make a **decision**

4. A purchase is made (**action**)

This process may take days, weeks or months for big purchases or it can be almost instantaneous for little purchases like getting a Coke from the vending machine...but it happens in every single purchase.

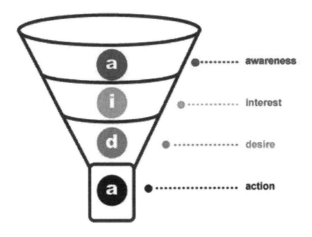

The level in the process in which someone finds themselves is their buyer intent, how close they are to making a decision.

The biggest problem in keyword research, even for bloggers that spend a lot of time finding keywords with high-volume traffic and for which they can rank, is that few bloggers spend any time thinking about buyer intent.

Think about it. Which would you rather attract to your blog, a thousand visitors just looking for information on a product or 100 visitors that want to buy right now and just want to find the best product for their needs?

The way you manage these visitors, attracting the right ones to make more sales, is by ranking for keywords that show buyer intent.

It's not to say that articles around building awareness for a solution or product are worthless. You should have articles like these on your blog to give readers a complete view of the topic from start to finish. These types of articles can be a great way to get people into your email list, building that relationship and trust for when they are ready to make a purchase.

Keywords typical to the awareness and interest stage of buyer intent are also usually less competitive than others as well.

Some examples of Awareness and Interest keywords:

- Any search around getting general information
- Symptoms
- How do I
- How [product] is made
- Free [product]
- Types of [product]

Your best traffic though, the visitors that really make you money, is going to be to posts optimized for a keyword that signals high buyer intent. These are keywords that people in the decision and action stage use when they search. They already know what type of product they need and may even know the brands they want to buy.

Examples of Decision and Action Keywords:

Buyer intent keywords often have verbs in them or help a searcher find the best option at the right price

Get	Best	Deals
Buy	Top 10	Coupons
Subscribe	Affordable	Free Shipping
Discount	Price	Comparison
Where can I buy [product]		Review

Source: MyWorkfromHomeMoney.com

The downside to focusing on keywords that signal high buyer intent is that they are generally more competitive…duh. Bloggers and companies are going to be going after these keywords because they bring traffic that makes more money.

That doesn't mean you can't rank for these terms though, it just means you need to find less competitive keywords that have both volume and buyer intent.

What is Long-tail Keyword Research?

Just one last concept before getting to the keyword research process that will get you the Google love to be successful.

Everyone wants to rank on the first page of Google for the term 'make money' but we already saw that it's not going to happen unless you run a mega-site like Forbes or the Huffington Post. The keyword gets tens of thousands of monthly visitors and even a percentage of it could mean big time blog traffic.

But it's just a pipe dream for 99% of bloggers.

The answer is what's called long-tail keywords. These are phrases three- and four-words long that are far less competitive and will ultimately mean more traffic because you'll actually rank on the first page.

Look at these five Google searches:

- Make money online
- Make money blogging
- Make money online with real estate
- How do I make money fast?
- What is the best way to make money?

All five include the keyword 'make money' and contribute to the super-high search volume it gets every month. Two of the five include the term 'make money online' which is another high-volume keyword but not as high as the shorter term.

The longer searches like 'make money online with real estate' are going to have much fewer bloggers going after it because there will be fewer people searching the term every month. That means you'll have less competition to rank the keyword.

Did you notice another important idea in the list of five keyword searches?

There's a huge range in what the search is trying to find. Why would you spend so much time optimizing a post and going through so much SEO work to rank for the term 'make money.' Unless you covered virtually every way to make money in the post, a lot of your visitors are going to be disappointed.

Looking for good long-tail keyword ideas in your research will not only help you find terms for which you can rank on the first page of Google but will also help give your readers a better experience by finding the information they need.

How to Start Keyword Research for a Blog Post

I hope you're still with me because now we get to the actual keyword research process and the free keyword tools I use to rank every post.

Using this keyword research process will add 15 or 20 minutes to each post but it can mean a huge bump in traffic and thousands more visitors every month.

Here's the keyword research process in a nutshell:

1. Brainstorm keywords on the post topic and the article goals
2. Use Google drop-down and related search suggestions
3. Use Google Adwords suggested keywords and 'Get Ideas' from KWP
4. Look for linked words on the topic Wikipedia page
5. Look for sub-Reddits and group questions
6. Narrow your list by monthly search impressions
7. Narrow your list by buyer intent
8. Use the MozBar extension to find less competitive keywords

Start out the keyword process by brainstorming a few higher-level keyword ideas. What is the broad topic covered in the post and what questions does it answer? What do you want readers to learn or do after reading the post?

If you were searching for the topic, how would you search in Google? Brainstorm a list.

I will often write up a post or at least develop a detailed outline before doing keyword research. Then I go back and see what words or phrases show up the most. This helps me find keyword ideas that occur naturally in the content.

After doing your full keyword research process, you can go back through and do a quick rewrite or just place your exact keyword into sections of the post. You'll also be able to place synonyms and related keywords within the post, both very important as signals to Google on keyword ranking.

Too many bloggers have a keyword they want to target before writing a post and then just try to stuff it in the writing. It leads to a clunky reader experience and Google penalizes the page because the keyword isn't natural.

Best Free Keyword Research Tools

After putting together a quick list of ideas, I'll run to several free keyword research tools on the web. There are also paid tools available, many that do other tasks like competitor research and link-building, but you'll get everything you need with the keyword tools below.

- Google search drop-down is simply typing in your keyword ideas and seeing what Google suggests as you type. These are going to be very popular searches with high traffic but may also be very competitive. Take the drop-down idea one step farther with Soovle, a site that shows drop-down suggestions for all the search engines at once.

- Google related search suggestions are displayed at the bottom of the search page and can be a great keyword resource for longer-tail ideas

- Google Adwords suggest reveals a lot of keyword ideas. Go to the Keyword Planner Tool and then Campaigns. Start a new campaign and copy the URL to a similar page on a competitor's blog where it says 'Enter your Landing Page'. You'll need to enter a starting bid and daily budget but you won't be actually starting this campaign so don't worry about spending any money.

Google will scan the landing page you entered and suggest keywords related to the page.

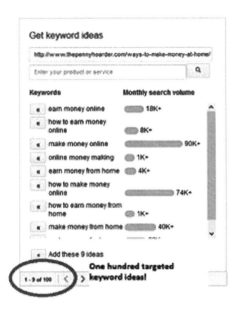

- Another resource is the Google Keyword Planner tool itself. Log in to your Adwords account and go to the keyword planner. Click on the 'Search for new keywords using a phrase, website or category. It's not a requirement but I like to change the filters for monthly searches above 500 and high competition. Make sure you target for your location and language.

The result will be a huge list, usually into the hundreds of keyword ideas with monthly search volume. I like to download the list into Excel which makes it easier to add my other keyword ideas.

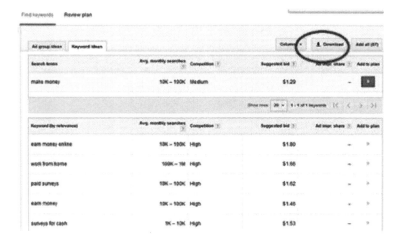

- One free keyword research tool that few people use is Wikipedia. Go to the Wiki page for your broad topic and look through it for linked words, those highlighted in blue and clickable. This is going to give you a list of related words and the Contents box is a great resource for sub-level keywords.

- Reddit can also be used to find keyword ideas. Search for your post topic to find sub-Reddits and look through the forum titles to see common questions and keywords that people use frequently.

- Finally, UberSuggest is another free keyword tool that generates hundreds of keyword ideas. You won't need to copy down all the suggestions but browse through the list to pick out any ideas that sound relevant.

These seven free keyword tools will give you hundreds of ideas and it takes less than 10 minutes to run through them all. You may not need to use every resource for every blog post but make sure you build a good list of potential keywords.

Narrowing the Keyword List for your Blog Post

With this initial list of keyword ideas, head over to the Google Keyword Planner again and paste them into the 'Get search volume data and trends' box. This will give you the monthly searches, competition and suggested bid for each keyword.

I usually will delete any keyword ideas with less than 500 or 1,000 monthly searches but you may want to keep a few lower volume ideas if there aren't much higher-volume options.

You will also want to sort the list by the competition score (1.0 is high) and by suggested bid. Something most bloggers get wrong is that the competition score is not the difficulty in ranking the keyword, it's the relative number of people bidding on the term in Adwords.

High competition and high suggested bid keywords are important because they often signal a high level of buyer intent...why else would a lot of Adwords bidders be willing to pay a high price for the keyword? You also want to browse through the list for any action words or keywords that sound like a person would be close to making a buying decision.

After this, you should have a list of at least 10 to 20 potential keywords. Next you are going to see how easy it will be to rank each of these keywords and select one for your post.

Open up Google Chrome for your internet browser. Yeah, I like FireFox better as well but Chrome has some great extensions that are must-haves for bloggers. You can still use another browser for 'net surfing but you want to use Chrome for your keyword research.

Install the MozBar extension by searching for it on Google and clicking install. This is going to give you all kinds of great SEO clues when you do a search. Type in each of your short-list keyword ideas individually to see ranking details.

There are three things you will look at to determine keyword difficulty and whether you have a chance of ranking for a keyword.

- Page Authority (PA) is the most important. Google ranks pages, not domains though a site's overall domain authority will affect the PA.

- Domain Authority (DA) is still important because higher authority domains will find it easier to boost their PA.

- Links are a big factor in page authority besides all the on-page factors we'll cover in the next chapter. Even if a page has a lower PA, it can still rank for a keyword if it has a lot of quality links to it.

You can find your own website's domain authority by clicking over to the Moz Open Site Explorer (Moz OSE) or using any number of free tools on the web. The page authority for a post will differ depending on the number of inbound links and other factors.

I like to average the PA for the top five pages on Google. You are looking for which keywords in your list will be most easily ranked.

- Average PA of under 35 will be easy to rank

- Average PA between 35 and 50 can rank with a full SEO Process

- Average PA between 50 and 60 will be harder to rank and you'll need serious SEO

- Average PA above 60 and you better be Forbes if you want to rank

Once you've found one keyword idea that has good search volume, high buyer intent and is not too competitive to rank…you're ready to put it into your post.

Don't trash your list of potential keywords for the post. You will want to use some of these in place of your main keyword so it doesn't look like you're stuffing one keyword into your post. You will also want to use a few of these as your anchor text in guest posts to link back to the article.

If Google sees one anchor text linking back to a post, it may assume you are trying to manipulate the rankings. Use some related variations though and you'll have a better chance of ranking many different keywords.

What the Keyword Research Process Means for Your Blog

If you aren't ranking on the first page of Google then you aren't getting the traffic you need to be really successful. You might get some traffic here and there but it's a trickle of what you could be getting.

You don't want a traffic trickle…you want a traffic firehose for every single post!

It's why we focus most of our competitive research on the first page. Even the tenth result in a Google search typically only gets 2% of the clicks so you can imagine what ranking on the second or third page means.

In fact, I would rather rank first on Google for a keyword that only gets 500 monthly searches than ranking #10 for a keyword that gets ten-times as many searches!

As an example, I used data on the percentage of clicks each spot on Google typically gets to show how much traffic you can expect for keywords with different search volume.

What's the Top Spot Worth?

Google Traffic to Page by Rank and Monthly Searches

	Monthly Searches				
	500	1,000	5,000	10,000	50,000
1	163	325	1,625	3,250	16,250
2	88	176	880	1,760	8,800
3	57	114	570	1,140	5,700
4	41	81	405	810	4,050
5	31	61	305	610	3,050
6	22	44	220	440	2,200
7	18	35	175	350	1,750
8	16	31	155	310	1,550
9	13	26	130	260	1,300
10	12	24	120	240	1,200

Rank in Google Search Results (row labels 1–10)

Source: MyWorkfromHomeMoney.com
Traffic is approximate based on Chitika 2013 study.

The top spot for a keyword with just 500 monthly searches can send you 163 visitors a month, more than the #10 ranked page for a keyword that gets 5,000 monthly searches. Understand too that those high-volume keywords that are getting 5k, 10k and 50,000 searches are extremely competitive and you probably won't even be able to get on the first page.

This strategic use of keywords will make all the difference for your blog. Using a keyword research process that includes buyer intent, competition and search volume will not only help you rank on Google but will make sure you're getting the kind of traffic that makes you money. Take the extra 15 minutes to run through this keyword process for every post and you'll be out ahead of nearly every other blogger.

How to Write for Google Love

After you know what keyword you want to rank for, you can begin the writing process and use on-page SEO to highlight the post for Google.

What? You thought writing a blog post was only about writing something that will interest readers?

The entire SEO process is about telling Google that a post is important and how important it is for people searching the internet.

On-page SEO is the first part of that process, getting Google to sit up and notice your post for the keywords you want to target. Off-page SEO is the process of telling Google 'how' important your post is and will include most of the chapters after this one.

On-page SEO will get you immediate traffic from Google and it's one of the steps in our process most within your control.

That makes it a huge opportunity for bloggers.

What is On-Page SEO?

Getting visitors from online search is about understanding what search engines like Google do and how they work. Google wants to highlight the very best and most relevant information every time someone searches for a keyword. If people are happy with the results they find when using Google, they'll come back to the search engine and that adds up to big advertising money for the company.

Since Google uses a computer program to rank websites for search, it can't make qualitative judgments by reading an article. It has to find the best quality and relevant articles by other means.

Instead, Google looks at other signals like the words used in an article and readers' reactions when they land on the website. Link-building website Backlinko estimates that there are more than 200 factors Google looks at for website ranking.

That's where on-page SEO comes in. On-page SEO refers to how you set up a blog post to tell Google what the post is about and what keywords it should focus on in ranking.

General On-Page SEO Ranking Factors

There are some general things to do in your writing for on-page SEO success and some more specific ranking factors which we'll get to later in the chapter. The idea is that you want your blog post to stand out to Google for your targeted keyword.

New blogs aren't going to rank for very competitive keywords but you can make a run at longer phrases. You can also use modifiers like "best" and the year to attach to your keyword, making it easier to rank on Google.

Instead of just stuffing your keyword phrase into the article dozens of times, something Google is wise to and penalizing articles, use similar words to boost your relevancy. If I'm trying to rank for "on-page SEO checklist" I can also use phrases like "on-page SEO practices" and "SEO ranking list".

Most of the time, your keyword and similar phrases are going to appear naturally when you write about a topic but it always helps to go back through after you're done and fit some keywords in where you can.

Linking to Your Previous Blog Posts

Internal linking is another big factor in our on-page SEO checklist for multiple reasons. This is where you link to other pages and posts on your blog from the article.

By linking to other posts with keyword phrases for which you want those posts to rank, you're telling Google that those targets are important for those keywords. You also help Google find all the posts on your site by creating something like a map of links.

Just be sure not to use the same keyword to link to your older post that you're trying to rank for the article you're writing. Google won't know which post is more important for that keyword. We'll cover more of this idea in the next chapter and one of my favorite content strategies, the hub-and-spoke strategy.

How Long Should Your Blog Articles Be?

The average blog post is just under 800 words long. That's not bad, a little more than a page and a half should give you time to include some good information for Google to pick up on.

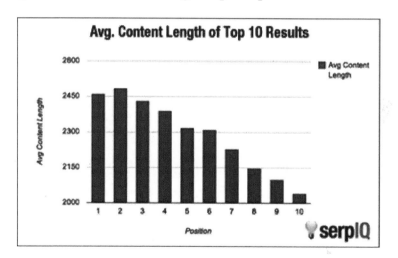

Too bad most of these posts don't have a chance of ranking.

SerpIQ surveyed the first page results on Google, clicking through and noting the word length on each. It found the average content length of top posts were all over 2,000 words and the top three results averaged 2,400 words.

Remember, Google is a computer so it's not playing favorites. There are good reasons why longer articles rank better on search engines.

1. Longer articles include more opportunities to hit on an easy keyword phrase. One of the best surprises in blogging is writing a long article and having it rank for many different keywords. The keyword phrase you build into your on-page SEO list is the one you're targeting but you might also rank for a range of other phrases if the article provides lots of information.

2. Longer articles offer more in-depth information and have more opportunities for getting links. Other bloggers want to provide info to their readers. Which is easier, linking to a huge resource guide or trying to write it up yourself? Those inbound links from other websites are pure gold for ranking on Google.

3. Finally, longer articles keep readers on your page longer...duh! Google can't read an article and rank it on quality. It has to look at readers' reactions and one important marker is how long someone stays on a page. Keep a reader on the page longer and get them clicking to other pages on your site and Google will assume the reader found what they wanted.

After 18 months of blogging, I looked through my ranking data to see which posts were ranking best. I had always tried to post twice a week to each blog to give readers a constant stream of information and to give Google something to index. The results were an eye-opener and changed the way I blogged afterwards.

	PeerFinance101		Crowd101		My Stock Market Basics	
	Average Word Count	% Total Traffic	Average Word Count	% Total Traffic	Average Word Count	% Total Traffic
Top Post	4,827	31%	3,979	39%	2,254	47%
Top 5 Posts	3,454	55%	2,878	52%	2,212	64%
Top 10 Posts	2,793	60%	2,401	63%	3,744	69%

Source: PeerFinance101, Crowd101, My Stock Market Basics.

The table shows the average word count on ranking posts across three blogs. My average word count on all posts was just over 1,000 words but the posts actually getting search traffic were much longer.

In fact, the best performing posts on the blogs were well over 2,000 words and accounted for nearly two-thirds of my total traffic.

This doesn't mean that every post you write needs to be 2,000+ words but the posts you really want to rank should detail out the topic completely. For you, it may mean posting just once a week or even once a month with a super-long, detailed article rather than more often smaller posts. Focus on quality articles and you will be rewarded with search traffic.

Google is smarter than you know and its ranking program evolves every year. You don't need to know all the details of the program to be successful, just understand that the more natural you make an article and the better information you provide will go a long way to start your ranking process.

Your On-page SEO Checklist for Every Article

Beyond the general factors to improve your SEO ranking on Google, there are some very important specific things you can do on every article. Follow this on-page SEO checklist to get your articles started right and get that Google love.

Again, it all comes back to your keyword and the signals you send to Google. When I say 'keyword' I mean the keyword phrase for which you're trying to rank, not necessarily just one word. One of the most important factors in on-page SEO ranking is where you use your keyword in the article.

- **Title** – There's something to be said for catchy titles that draw readers but if it doesn't include your keyword then Google doesn't know what the article is about. It helps if you can get the keyword in first but just anywhere in your title is a good start.

- **URL**– This is the website address of your article and usually automatically created from your title. I usually change this to only the keyword phrase with hyphens separating each word. This lets Google know that the post is focused on exactly that keyword. You don't want to target the same keyword on more than one post so you shouldn't have to worry about duplicate URLs on your blog.

- **Headline** – This is one-sentence at the top of your article that tells readers what it's about and why it's important. You want to change the headline to an H2 tag by highlighting the text and clicking the drop-down box shown in the image below. These H-tags are important coding signals to Google that the text is important. H1 is your title, while H2 is more important than H3 and so on.

- **First and last paragraphs** – You don't absolutely need your keyword phrase in the first and last paragraphs but it should be in the first and last 100 words. Google figures that you are setting up the topic and then summarizing in these two spots so any keywords found are going to be important to the article.

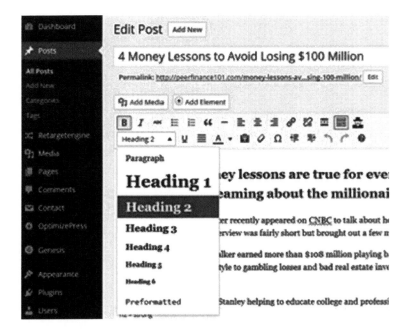

- **Section headings** – I'm always surprised when I get a guest post by someone that is just one long block of writing. You need to break your article up into at least two or more sections, each section around an idea. It helps organize your article and gives readers a break on longer posts…and it also gives you an opportunity to give another on-page SEO signal to Google by including your keyword phrase and tagging the heading with an H3 tag.

- **Images** – Google can't look at a picture or graphic to see if it adds to the article quality. Google has to rely on other signals like the file name of the image, the description and alternative tag. Make sure you include at least one relevant image in each post and include your keyword in the tags and file name. You'll do this when you save the image on your computer and upload it to WordPress.

- **Meta description** – The meta description is the brief couple of sentences that Google shows on each search result. Google says the meta description doesn't matter for SEO but it does matter indirectly. The percentage of people that click on your post in search results, called the click-through-rate (CTR), is a signal to Google that your post answered their search need. You boost your CTR with an exciting and engaging meta description. If you have the Yoast SEO plug-in on your blog, you'll write out your description at the bottom of the page in WordPress.

Finally, make sure to include your keyword and similar words throughout the content. Don't feel like you have to repeat the same phrase over and over but your keyword phrase should appear several times if the article is truly about the topic.

A lot of bloggers are stingy with their outbound links. They don't want to send readers anywhere but to internal pages on their blog. It's a big mistake and won't help you make any friends in the blogoverse.

Linking to high authority websites in your article is also a signal to Google that the article provides quality information to readers. I always try to link to one outside source to give readers extra info on a related topic. Just be sure not to use your target keyword as the outbound link or Google may think that page is more important than yours for the phrase.

We've already talked about how longer articles keep readers on your site and why it's important. There's another way to do this by using different forms of media in your posts, stuff like videos and infographics. Not only will other media types engage your readers but they'll also attract more links to your article.

Social sharing plug-ins are an important part of your on-page SEO checklist because they help provide the off-page social signals to Google. I like the Shareaholic plugin because it provides floating share buttons, buttons that stay on the screen as the reader scrolls, and doesn't slow down your website too much.

Not only is social sharing on Facebook, Twitter and other networks going to bring more readers to your blog but Google will see this interaction as a sign of quality.

Writing for Search Snippets

Google has rolled out a new project over the last couple of years and it's become a huge opportunity for bloggers. Search snippets are the quick answer box you see at the top of Google results, before any organic results but after the ads.

These search snippets appear on about a fifth of searches now but the trend is to more. While everyone tries to rank in the first search result...search snippets amount to search result #0 and can mean a big traffic boost.

One of the best reasons to optimize your posts for search snippets is because Google doesn't always pull from the top results. While most posts highlighted in search snippets rank on the first page, it may be from #3 or #5 and give you a chance to appear twice on the page.

When you're writing a post, or republishing a popular post, create a section or two on popular questions people use to search for the topic. Summarize the answer to the question in a few bullet points and consider including a table that compares different solutions.

One problem with search snippets is that a reader may answer their question directly off Google and not need to click through to your site.

Google usually includes three or four points in its search snippet box. This means you can increase your chance of getting a click by highlighting more points in the process. Don't boil the answer down to just three points. Reference five points in the description and put all five in your bullets.

On-page SEO is incredibly important to your success as a blogger and surprisingly, not that difficult. It's one of the few steps in the complete SEO process that is entirely within your control and will help you rank each post you write.

The Hub-and-Spoke Blogging Strategy

So we know that links to your posts are hugely important to getting found in search. Links are a big part of how Google finds your posts to index in search results.

The problem is that getting inbound links from other sites can take weeks and even then it will take Google time to find those links.

Unless Google is crawling your blog constantly, usually only something that happens for the very large sites that post daily or more, then your posts aren't going to be showing up in search for a while.

What if I told you one of the best sources for links is one you control?

Not only will this linking strategy help Google find its way around your blog to different posts but it will also help create a better reader experience, it's a win-win for everyone.

How Internal Linking Makes for Stronger SEO

We talked very briefly about internal linking in the last chapter but I wanted to save the detail for this one because it fits perfectly with one of my favorite content strategies.

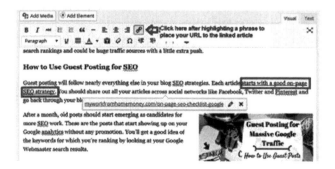

Let's start off with the power of internal linking, simply highlighting a word or phrase in a blog post and making it clickable to another page or post on your blog.

Internal linking through the strategy we'll detail below is going to do three things for your blog:

1. It makes it easier for Google to find its way around your site. Google's spiders crawl through a post and linked posts. Using internal links in your posts and pages makes sure that Google finds everything on your site faster.

2. Internal links give people something else to read and more detailed information. This makes for a better reader experience. It also improves your search ranking through lower bounce rate and more pages per visitor, two factors Google loves.

3. Your links help establish the importance of posts for specific keywords. Your blog may be about 'underwater basket weaving' but which post is the best for 'underwater basket weaving on horseback?' Link your articles so Google can send people to your best work.

The beauty of internal linking is that it's quick and easy. It takes seconds to link to an older article and not much more time to go back through older posts and link new articles.

Internal Linking Posts while Writing for SEO Power

I keep a spreadsheet of all my articles with a one-sentence description and keywords. Within this list is a column marked for the posts that have a real shot at ranking for high-traffic keywords. These are super-detailed posts I call my 'hub' articles.

Think of your SEO strategy as a wheel with one hub in the center and several spokes coming out to the edge of the wheel. The hub articles are those strong posts that you want to target for Google search ranking.

Hub-and-Spoke Blogging Strategy

Source: MyWorkfromHomeMoney.com

Hub articles are:

- Strong long-form content (> 2,000 words) with lots of detail
- Targeted for a high-traffic keyword and hit every box in our on-page SEO checklist
- Have a strong call-to-action like email subscription or to a money-making strategy like an affiliate

Whenever I write an article that references a topic covered by one of these hub articles, I include a link. It tells Google the hub article is really important for the topic and it gives readers every opportunity to find it.

I'm actually more strategic than that in my blogging strategy. When I plan a hub article, I will also plan at least a few smaller spoke articles that complement it. The spoke articles are usually smaller volume but less competitive variations of my hub article keyword.

Since the keywords are related, Google sees the hub and spoke articles as related and they share more SEO juice when you link them. The spoke article may be smaller but can draw some strong traffic on a less competitive keyword and then send some of that traffic to the hub article.

Why not make every article 'hub' quality? Are all your articles 2,000+ words long and painstaking quality?

It doesn't mean that you slack on all of your spoke articles but there are just some article ideas that are going to turn into mega-posts with enough information to make Merriam-Webster jealous.

Besides your intentional 'hub' articles, you also want to keep an eye on Google Webmaster and analytics for the blog. SEO is weird and sometimes an article will just rank for a keyword even without doing much for it. You might want to change some of your 'spoke' articles to hubs if they are ranking really well for a keyword and bringing you traffic.

I've included a chapter on using Google Webmaster next to show you how to use this excellent SEO tool.

Whenever I'm updating my list of posts, I also note the number of times I've linked to an article. You'll want to throw a few links to your spoke articles as well to make it easier for Google to find them.

Going Back to Internally-Link Posts

Placing internal links while you're writing a new post is easy. You start writing about a topic and…"hey, I remember I've got another post about that."

More difficult but still worth your time is going back through older posts to internally link your new articles. That's where the spreadsheet of all your posts comes in handy to help find posts in which to place your new links.

I try linking every post in at least two older posts and try linking 'hub' or targeted articles in at least two or three older posts. Remember, it's not just about Google finding it and the SEO signals but about making your best content as easy as possible to find for readers.

Two final tips on placing internal links:

- Don't link to an article with the same keyword phrase every time. This goes for your off-page SEO as well. Google will see this as artificial and a kind of keyword manipulation and will ding the ranking for a post. Have a list of three or four related keyword phrases you use for your links on each post.

- Don't link a post for the same keyword for which you are trying to rank the post you're writing. Example: If you're writing a post about 'exploring Uranus' don't link to another post using the exact clickable keyword. You don't want Google to be guessing which post is most important for 'exploring Uranus'.

Because internal linking is so easy to do and so important for your blog's overall SEO health, it's one of the can't-miss things you need to do regularly. While other SEO strategies like guest posting take longer and may be something you only do for really important posts, you can internally link your blog quickly and really boost your search rankings.

Using My Favorite SEO Tool: Google Webmaster

I'm going to take a quick break from the Google SEO process to talk about my favorite SEO tool and how it will help you rank higher in search.

The tool is the Google Webmaster site, now called the Search Console, and it's a must for bloggers…and completely free.

What is the Google Search Console?

Yeah, sorry. I still call it Google Webmaster but the name was officially changed to Search Console in 2015.

The search console is a free service to website owners that lets you check a huge range of SEO and technical issues on your sites.

- Submit a sitemap that helps Google find its way around your blog
- Make sure Google is crawling your site and finding pages
- See a list of internal links and links coming from other websites
- See keywords that each post is ranking for along with the position in Google
- See if Google is penalizing your site for any reason

We will focus on the SEO-related tools like checking your rankings for a post and getting a list of links.

How to Set up Google Search Console for your Blog

You will need a Google account to access the Search Console but that's a fairly easy process. Once you've got an account, go to the search console and click the 'Add a Property' button.

You'll then see a box asking for your website URL including http. After copying your blog URL and hitting 'Add', it will take you to a page with an HTML tag.

The code starts off with <meta name=… but you only need to copy the section within the parenthesis.

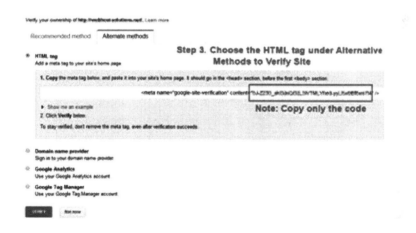

Login to WordPress and go to your Yoast plugin in the left-hand menu. It's labeled SEO in the menu with a Y logo beside it.

In the Webmaster Tools tab of Yoast, you'll find the box where you paste your verification code next to Google Search Console.

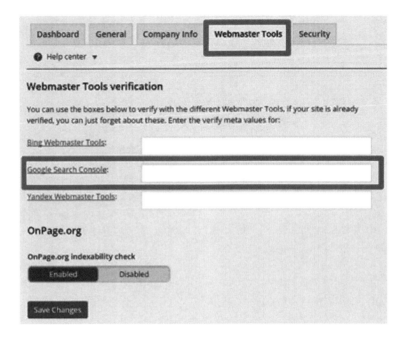

Go back to the Search Console and hit verify. That's it.

Using the Search Console SEO Super-Tool

When you login to your Search Console, you'll see a menu on the left and the current status for crawl errors, analytics and sitemaps.

Let's start with my favorite, Search Analytics. You can get there in the menu under Search Traffic and then clicking on Search Analytics.

This page gives you a ton of information. You can check any or all of the boxes to show clicks, impressions, CTR or keyword position and use the toggles to filter for a number of choices.

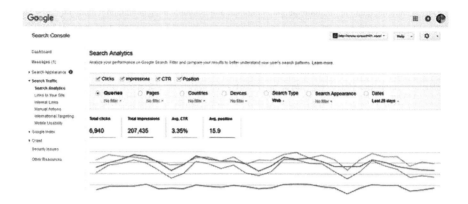

With the 'Queries' button toggled, you'll see all the searches for which your blog ranks. Impressions is how many times one of your pages showed up for that search term while clicks are the amount of visitors you got from it.

Clicks divided by impressions is your click-through-rate and an important signal to Google that people saw what they wanted when your page was shown. Position is the average search ranking during the period.

Seeing the site-wide queries is interesting but I like to toggle for 'Pages' first to see each page.

	Pages	Clicks ▼	Impressions	CTR	Position
1	/list-crowdfunding-and-fundraising-websites/	2,766	101,046	2.74%	12.2
2	/list-crowdfunding-and-fundraising-websites/amp/	431	16,790	2.57%	8.4
3	/19-ways-to-promote-your-crowdfunding-campaign/	491	3,663	10.95%	11.8
4	/church-fundraising-ideas-to-crowdfund/	358	11,556	3.1%	22.5
5	/crowdfunding-promotion-scam/	347	5,554	6.25%	14.4
6	/top-5-crowdfunding-platforms-equity-investing/	215	5,424	3.96%	16.6
7	/church-fundraising-ideas-to-crowdfund/amp/	141	1,645	8.57%	10.7

This will show the search traffic and ranking for each individual page on your blog...but it gets even better.

Click on one of the page URLs and then toggle the 'Queries' filter again. This will show you the keywords for which that page is ranking.

	Queries	Clicks ▼	Impressions	CTR	Position
1	crowdfunding platforms	109	3,412	3.19%	7.4
2	crowdfunding websites	74	4,703	1.57%	8.6
3	crowdfunding sites	50	3,283	1.52%	8.7
4	best fundraising sites	48	673	7.13%	4.3
5	fundraising platforms	48	499	9.62%	3.0
6	best crowdfunding sites	29	2,146	1.35%	8.2

This is a gold-mine of SEO information and we'll be referring back to it frequently through the rest of the book.

- Sort the information by impressions to see which keywords might have high-volume but for which you might not yet be ranking highly or getting many clicks.

- Sort by position to see which keywords you are showing up on the first page.

- Check to see if the CTR for any pages is really low and might be improved by changing the page title or meta-description.

- Keywords with an average position from 7 to 12 might be good candidates for improvement. Move these keywords up just a couple rankings and you could get significantly more traffic.

You can also filter by country, device and search type but I don't use these much. You can change the date to show up to 90 days of information and the tool is great for comparing changes to your search power.

Another handy tool for SEO is the 'Links to Your Site' page which shows the other websites that link to your pages. Click 'Links to Your Site' in the left menu and then 'More' under the list of your most linked content or 'Who Links the Most'.

Not only will this show you sites linking to individual posts but you can also see if there are sites that regularly link to your blog. This is a huge resource for finding other bloggers that are most likely to give you another link when you come out with quality, new content.

There are a lot of other great tools in the Search Console but these are the two that you'll use most in your SEO process. Look around a little and get to know some of the other resources and how they can help you develop your blog.

Getting Search Going with Audio, Video and PDFs

To this point in our SEO process, we have mostly focused on creating great content around some target keywords. This is where a lot of bloggers quit the process. They work solely on writing and just hope that Google rewards them.

It's the easy road but leads nowhere.

If you really want to rank on Google and be successful, you have to go further. You have to actively get links from other websites.

Link-building can be a frustratingly slow process but is absolutely necessary if you ever want to rank on Google.

Fortunately, there are a few link-building strategies that can be done to get a ton of links with less work than it takes guest posting and getting on blog rolls. Among my favorite linking strategies is boosting website ranking through sharing different types of media formats.

I'm talking about converting a post or parts of your article into formats like pdf, video, audio and infographics. It doesn't involve writing any new content so it's faster than other link strategies but can boost your blog's rank in so many ways.

How to Use Different Media to Boost your Google Ranking

We'll get into how to create the different type of media formats and different sites that will give you a link later.

First, let's run through how to use different media on and off your blog to drive reader engagement and huge SEO power!

By creating different media from your post, you get the opportunity to make it more engaging to readers and can get lots of links fast. Any way you can provide your content in different ways, through graphics or video or audio, you are going to appeal to a larger range of people and you're going to get more links.

After creating your new media (more on this below), your first decision will be to add it to the existing post or to create another post. I usually prefer to add it to the old post to make it more interesting but you might not want all four media formats loaded into one post.

Creating another post with the new media and around a similar keyword phrase gives you the opportunity to rank two keywords instead of one. Just remember to internally link your new post to the old article using the target keyword phrase for which you want to rank.

After creating and adding the new media to your blog, you're next going to go off-site to share the media and get links back to the article.

Some of the sites below will give you dofollow links back to the article which are pure gold for website ranking though many will be nofollow links. Kinda sucks that all links aren't dofollow but even the nofollow links help to increase the article's link profile.

PDFs to Promote your Post and Boost your Blog Ranking

A pdf is like an electronic hard-copy of your post. These work great as downloadable offers on your blog to get people to subscribe to an email list or as an off-page link-building strategy.

If you are going to use a post as a downloadable pdf document, make sure it is truly something valuable and more than just a standard article. If a reader is going to take the time to download a document and open it, they want to see something they won't get in any other article on the site. Consider adding content, a list or some graphics to the content before you convert it into the pdf format.

Make sure you link content in your article to offers on your blog, other articles and the original article. These links will work in your pdf document and anyone that downloads it could find themselves back at your blog if they like what they see.

As with all the media formats here as well as sharing them around, you could do all the work yourself. It's going to take a few hours but I suggest you do it at least once yourself to set up accounts on the different linking sites and to get the feel of it. After once or twice, you might want to hire the work out to an assistant on Fiverr or through another freelancer site.

For $5 on Fiverr, you can find someone that will share your media files on many of the sites below. There are 128 file sharing sites listed below, though some are duplicated across different formats and some may go down over time.

Even if you only plan on sharing across half that many sites, it could take you a few hours to upload and share on them all.

There are plugins and paid tools to help you create a pdf document directly from a blog post but I've got an easier…and free solution.

I write up all my blog posts first in a Word document. I keep all my posts for each blog on one document and just keep adding on the bottom with the publication date. This gives me an easily searchable document for all the content on my blog and makes it easy to repurpose content into books and other formats.

From that single Word document with all my posts, all I have to do is copy/paste an article onto a separate document. Then I can 'Save As' and change the 'Save as Type' to pdf to automatically convert it to PDF.

An important step in creating all these different media formats is that you want to name the file around the keywords you are trying to target. Websites and Google read these file names and it's a big factor in website ranking.

Once your PDF is created, you can start sharing it around the web.

Remember to make your file 'public' when adding it to file sharing sites like Google Drive. This will allow anyone to find it and share it around.

There are a few things to remember when you're sharing your different media files, not just PDFs but all four of the media formats, that will drastically improve your blog ranking.

Sites to Link Your PDFs

2shared	ISSUU
4shared	KeepandShare
Calameo	MediaFire
crocodoc	MirrorCreator
DepositFiles	MultiUpload.biz
DocDroid	pdfcast.org
Docspal	Scribd
DocStoc	sharesend
dropbox	SlideShare
edocr	uploading
EmbedUpload	Wattpad
filedropper	Web Host Server
gazhoo	YouScribe
Google Drive	Ziddu

All sites .com unless noted otherwise

- Most sites allow you to write a description for the file. Make sure you use as much of this as possible to get your keyword in there and persuade people to look at the file. You also want to include the URL address of the article here because some sites will convert it to a live link that people can click.

- Make sure to include a link to the original article on the sharing site when you can and add tags the file with keywords.

- Take the time to create a real profile on each sharing site including an image and a link back to your blog homepage. These profile links are sometimes the only dofollow links allowed so they are definitely something you want to grab.

- Building a following on some of the file sharing sites takes time but can help your content get shared and go viral. It's a good job for a virtual assistant because you really just need to make a point of following others and 'liking' their content.

- Use multiple calls to action in all your media. These are special call-outs where you tempt people to click through to your blog for more details or special content. You want at least one within the first 30 seconds of viewing or reading to get those quick clickers but also want one around the middle of your content and one at the end.

- For PDFs and PowerPoint media, add callouts and links to other articles as well. Many sites will pick up on these links to create some SEO juice to your posts though some will not find links on the first three pages or slides (i.e. Slideshare).

Turn it into an Infographic for Link-worthy Content and Boosted Website Ranking

People are visual creatures and love any kind of graphic. Infographics used to be gold in getting links back to your blog. They've lost some of this power but are still much more effective at getting links than plain text articles.

Creating an infographic from a post is easier than you may think. Take a look at some of the most popular graphics on Pinterest, the ones getting tens of thousands of repins. How much actual content is there?

The best infographics really don't have that much content. Grab six to ten facts from your post, preferably ones that have some kind of numerical element. If visual graphics and design aren't your strong suit, search Pinterest for infographics related to your blog post for ideas on structure and how to represent the data.

You can create your own infographics in Powerpoint, Publisher or any number of graphic design packages. I've never been much of a graphics person so I just outsource all my infographics. The important point here is to have a clear idea and outline of what you want the infographic to look like, along with the exact text that will go in it. With that already done, you can usually get your graphics created for less than $40 on Fiverr or through another freelancing site.

Infographic sizes can vary but generally around 600 to 900 pixels wide and three or four times than in length work best for web and mobile viewing.

Once you've got your infographic created, you can either add it to the original blog post or create another post. If your original blog post is already long-form content over 2,000 words, you might want to just create another post and internally link to the original. Adding your graphic to an already long post risks that people won't see your graphic if it's at the end of the post.

Whichever you decide, make sure to create an embed code like the one on SiegeMedia. An embed code is html that will put a box under your infographic with code that people can copy and put on their own blog. This makes it easier for others to share your infographic and provides an instant link back to your article.

There are more infographic sharing sites than for any other media. Some have extremely high page rank and domain authority and great visitor traffic.

There's another use for different media formats that has worked very well for me, especially when creating an infographic around the info in your post. You can offer the infographic as part of a guest post to other bloggers. It gives you the opportunity to offer something more than a traditional guest post and usually gets a higher acceptance rate than just any guest post request.

Sites to Link Your Infographics

Visual.Ly	Dailystatistic	Infographiclist
Slideshare	Bestinfographics	Easel.ly
Infographicsshowcase	omginfographics	Infographicsite
infographicsarchive	nfogfx	Infographicas
Reddit.com/r/infographics	Infographicjournal	Pureinfographics
Nerdgraph	Flickr	Cloudinfographics
Loveinfographics	Visualising.org	Ratemyinfographic
Submitinfographics	Dailyinfographic	Infographicreviews
theinfographics.blogspot	Coolinfographic	Infographicsking
infographixdirectory	Styleandflow	Allinfographics.org
infographicsite	pdviz	
Infographaholic.tumblr	Infographiclabs	
Infographicpost	Amazinginfographics	
Infographicsonly	Vizualarchive	

All sites .com unless noted otherwise

Be a Star with Video and Boost your Website Ranking

Way back when, before anyone heard of Facebook, people where sharing their social lives on blogs. They started as just text content before the podcasting revolution took many into an audio format.

With the advent of YouTube and now the popularity of Facebook Live, it looks like the next evolution will be in video.

You don't have to be a Spielberg or be as photogenic as Jennifer Aniston to be successful in video. People love to see their favorite blogger and know that they are more than just a faceless icon on the website. Video lets you get your personality out like text never can.

The easiest way to create a video is through your computer's internal camera though some of the bloggers I know that do video often have spent up to $500 on a camera. I just use my laptop and software that lets me record and edit the video. Most of these screen-capturing packages can also be used to create videos of presentations and tutorials.

The most popular video editing software, though pretty expensive, is Camtasia. It is unique in that it allows you to create in-video links that viewers can click through to your blog. If Camtasia is out of your budget at $300, I know a lot of people that use Screencast-o-Matic for a free solution.

The important point in creating your video is to not worry too much about perfection. You can spend hours editing a simple three-minute video…or you can put it together in half an hour.

Unless you are extremely compelling, most viewers are not going to stick around for more than three minutes so don't feel like you've got to fit the whole blog post into your video. The idea is to get the key points across without taking away the need for the viewer to click through for all the detail.

Put your video script and cues together on a large-font document to use as a prompt while you record. Talk through it a couple of times before recording just to get your flow down. When you go record your video, I've always leaned heavily to the side of just going through all the way…mistakes and all. Viewers don't mind little gaffes and stutters, it shows you're a real person.

If you do want to make a mistake-free video, make a little clap or click on each mistake and then wait a second to start over on that part of the script. Don't start at the beginning! You'll never make it all the way through perfectly.

In your editing software, you'll be able to see your mistakes because the audio graph will spike on your clap and the dead air space will help to see where to cut the video. Save your video as either MP4 or WMV format.

You can add your video back to the original post or just add it to off-page sites. YouTube is the obvious first stop and is the second most trafficked site after Google but don't neglect the other sites on the list for links and visitors back to your blog.

Sites to Link Your Videos

YouTube	Veoh
Vimeo	Tinypic
Dailymotion	esnips
Twitch	Vidmax
Liveleak	Flixya
Break	Dropshots
Metacafe	Vidivodo
Facebook	Clipshack
Vine	Sutree
Instagram	Vidipedia
Ustream	Vevo
Revver	VidiLife

All sites .com unless noted otherwise

Be Heard if not Seen with Audio for Google Ranking Love

Before typical internet speeds could handle as much video as we have today, people were using audio and podcasting to reach other senses beyond simple text. Personally, I've always preferred reading a post and find myself drifting off during podcasts but there's a huge group of people that loves listening to spoken-word audio every day.

It's a whole new audience you can reach while people are driving or doing daily chores away from the computer. Audio recording software is easier (cheaper) to come by than video software. Audacity is the most popular and will let you do about everything you need to for free.

As with video recordings, I like to make my audio files as quickly and easily as possible. I read through my script a couple of times and then record straight through, mistakes and all.

I like to make shorter audio clips, shorter than three minutes but feel free to make longer audio files to include more detail. Just remember to add your calls-to-action at the beginning and end by asking people to visit your blog. Save your file with the keywords you are targeting and as an MP3 format.

Sites to Link Your Audio Content

Clyp.it	Purevolume	Spotify
Soundcloud	4shared	Zippyshare
Vocaroo	Buzznet	Yourlisten
Reverbnation	Jukeboxalive	Dopetracks
Box	Depositfiles	Hotfile
Pandora	2shared	Soundcloud
Picosong	Mog	Mixcloud
Rapidshare	Midomi	Audioboo.fm
Filedropper	Grooveshark	Audioboom
Live365	Last.fm	Podomatic
Yottamusic	Bandcamp	Ziddu
Finetune	Blip.fm	Audiomack
Buzzsprout	Tindeck	

All sites .com unless noted otherwise

Link-building with these four media formats is some of the easiest SEO you'll find in our process. You might not do all four formats with every post you publish but try doing at least an audio or video for each post and upload regularly to sharing sites.

It's here that you are going to be creating the initial momentum for your search ranking. You'll be drawing a lot of visitors from different sites and will be sending some great signals to Google for SEO.

Google Authority with Guest Posting

A lot of bloggers try guest posting as a way to draw new visitors to their site but the real benefit in writing for other bloggers is in the SEO value.

I get almost 1,200 visitors a month on one post because I used this strategy. I get search visitors on more than 55 keyword phrases for the post and it's not even a highly relevant topic for my blog.

That's more than a thousand visitors every month and I haven't done anything with the post in more than seven months.

It takes time to write up quality guest posts so you might not use it to boost every post you publish but don't get lazy. If you want a post to rank for a competitive keyword, you need to boost it with a few guest posts.

How to Use Guest Posting for SEO

Guest posts are articles you write for another blog and include a link to your website either in the content or in a bio section at the end. Guest posting on legit blogs with decent domain authorities will mean a lot more SEO juice for each link compared to some of the weaker links you get from file sharing or other methods.

Most bloggers make the mistake of only including a link to their homepage in a bio section at the end of the guest post. This is one of the biggest mistakes you can make. Plenty of websites are going to link to your homepage when they refer to your site. Take the opportunity in guest posts to boost specific pages with in-content links.

Besides the fact that in-content links give a stronger signal to Google, you also get the chance to tag the link with anchor text (the text that is linkable) with your keyword or a related keyword. This tells the search engine that the article linked to from that text is important for that idea.

Not all bloggers will allow an in-content link but many will if it is to a post that includes important information about the article's topic. That your most important articles should have some important (link-worthy) data or information is a given so this shouldn't be too much of a problem.

The Secret to Guest Post SEO Success

Most bloggers just blast out an email to every blogger address they have, asking for a guest post on the site.

That's going to get you a guest post on about one-in-ten blogs, tops.

To really get your posts on as many blogs as possible, you need to develop a relationship with bloggers first. They need to know that you're not just another commercial blog, spamming out emails.

Take a month to put together a list of blogs on which you want to post, legit blogs with strong domain authority. Follow their blog, share on social media and leave legitimate comments on their articles.

And for cryin' out loud, read their guest post policy. They may only allow a link in the bio section or may require a certain word limit. If

I'm going to take the time to write a quality guest post, I usually want to get two in-content links so I may put a blog at the bottom of the list if the guest policy says otherwise.

While you're on their site, check out a few guest posts to see if they allow in-content links and if all links are dofollow by right-clicking on the link and select Inspect Element (Q). Any link marked 'nofollow' will be worthless for SEO value.

After following them for a month, commenting on posts and sharing on social media, reaching out to the bloggers on your list will be the easy part. Send a short email asking if you can write a guest post.

- Describe your blog in one sentence, something so they know it's a blog and not a commercial website.

- Acknowledge their guest post rules by pointing out that your post will be a certain length, original content and any other requirements.

- Propose three topics for your post to give them a choice.

If you are sending out emails to many bloggers at once, make sure to use different guest post proposals. It's not impossible to write a few original articles around the same topic but it's easier if you can do different topics.

This process will get you a much better response rate, about one-in-four from my experience and really get your links out there.

While following a few bloggers before proposing a guest post will help, the best strategy is to become active in a larger blogger group around your topic. Find a couple of Facebook groups around your blog topic and interact with the community. Not only will this help you get guest posts but you'll also get links through roundup posts and occasional requests for advice.

Writing Guest Posts for SEO

Once you've been approved for a guest post on a blog, quality counts! You may want to write more guest posts for this blogger in the future so don't burn your bridges with crappy content.

Of course, it goes without saying that you should stick religiously to the blogger's guest post policy as you're writing.

The three topics you proposed in your outreach email should be related in some way to the post you want to boost, some way that you can refer to the post within the content.

So if I am planning on boosting a link about real estate investing in a guest post, I want to propose topics around investing or real estate. That way, I can include a paragraph that leads into the idea of real estate investing and drop my link in to give readers more information.

Of course, your guest post needs to be appropriate for the blogger's audience. If the blog is about crockpot meals, you aren't going to write a guest post about rewiring your house.

Read a few posts on the blogger's site and pay attention to any 'most popular' articles. Try to find at least one article that you can refer to and link in your post.

This is my favorite guest posting strategy, using one of the blogger's posts to spark a question that I weave in to the post topic. It integrates the guest post into the blog really well and helps to develop that relationship with the other blogger.

Make sure you alternate a couple of keyword phrases you use for the link you leave in guest posts. If Google sees a bunch of links on other sites but with the same anchor text, it may think you are trying to manipulate search ranking. Use a few related keyword phrases from your initial keyword research.

This is going to boost your post for each specific keyword but also for the overall general topic. Google's computer program has become extremely smart about its search ranking. It will rank a post for hundreds of related keywords if it ranks well for a related topic.

It's an added bonus if you can include a relevant image in with your guest post but it must be copyright free.

When you're emailing the post to the blogger, be sure to ask for an email when the post is live so you can share out on your social networks. Reaching your social network is half the benefit for the other blogger and will help you get another guest post in the future.

Finally, when the post is live, check to make sure your link is still included and that it's a dofollow link. The blogger may remove it or mark it nofollow but there's really nothing you can do about it. Just keep track of which blogs offer the opportunity for in-content links in the future.

Ranking a single article high on Google isn't an easy task, especially for some of your money-making, competitive keywords but it can be done. The trick is to follow an SEO ranking process that builds off-page inbound links to your strongest on-page SEO articles. Guest posting can be a great boost to search rankings and some of your strongest inbound links.

Making a Blog Rock with Link-building Strategies

Sometimes it seems bloggers spend money on all the wrong things to make a blog successful. Just about every blogger I know spends money on a social media management tool and many pay virtual assistants to help work through the mountain of emails they receive.

But very few spend money on link-building strategies, whether researching link opportunities or hiring a VA to do outreach, to help their blog grow.

It's too bad because there's good reason to believe that a link-building program will make a blog much stronger than the temporary traffic you get from social media.

I'm not talking about black hat link-building or the now-penalized spam links bloggers used to get away with but legit link-building that will boost your search ranking and drive tons of traffic to your blog.

Best yet, unlike guest posting which can take hours for each link, many of the link-building strategies here can be done on a much larger scale.

My Favorite Link-Building Strategies

Normally very secretive about its algorithm, Google has said that content and inbound links are the two most important factors for a page's search ranking.

It makes sense, right? Google wants to send people to quality pages that are closest to the info for which they were searching. A post with tons of information, measured in breadth and depth, is more likely to answer a reader's question. Inbound links are a confirmation of the quality of that content.

I'm not going to be the millionth person to tell you to write great content. Making a blog a great resource through content takes time and there's no way around it...unless you're willing to pay lots of money to hire quality writers.

Barring deep pockets, the faster way to make your blog stand out is by getting lots of inbound links to validate your content.

We've already covered a few link-building strategies like file sharing of pdf, video and audio as well as guest posting.

While file sharing works fast, most of the links aren't worth much because many will be nofollow. Guest posting links are dofollow but the process is very slow.

The best link-building strategies to grow a blog are the ones where you can get dozens and even up to hundreds of links quickly.

My favorite link-building strategies for making a blog jump in search and driving traffic are the skyscraper technique, infographics and scholarship pages.

Make a Blog Post Awesome with the Skyscraper Technique

This one comes from Brian Dean of the site Backlinko, an excellent resource for link-building techniques and ways to make a blog stand out. The skyscraper technique is the hardest and most labor-intensive of the strategies but really works to make awesome content and draw lots of inbound links to your blog.

Brian summarizes the skyscraper technique in three steps: finding link-worthy content, make something even better and then reaching out to the right people.

- Finding link-worthy content is easy, just search Google for the keywords for which you want to rank. Look through the top ten search results and really analyze the content. Why is it ranking so highly?

  o Is it visually great, meaning strong graphics or design?

  o Is it a huge resource, sharing hundreds of ideas and possible solutions to a reader's problem?

  o Does it share different perspectives, the pros and cons of the issue?

  o What's missing from the top ranking posts? Is there any topic within the keyword phrase that isn't addressed? Is some of the info from the top posts outdated?

- Make something better is just like it sounds. If you're going to compete for a broad keyword that gets lots of traffic, you better make an amazing resource.

  o Don't settle for the easy solution in a huge number post, i.e. 101 Ways to Make a Blog Grow. Don't get me wrong, your post can include a lot of list ideas but don't rely solely on the list to make your blog post shine. Add an infographic to it and try adding something more to the argument that's missing in other posts.

  o How big should your link-building post be? Research on the top ten posts in Google search shows an average word count above 2,000 words. Some of my highest ranked posts approach 5,000 words. It's no substitute for quality but size does seem to matter in making a blog post rank higher.

  o One of the best ways to do this is to start with existing content. It takes time to write super-content but it's a lot easier if you're already starting with a 1,000-word post with some great info.

- Reaching out to the right people is really the driver behind the skyscraper and all link-building strategies. Your super-content will eventually draw links and put your blog in search but giving it a push through outreach will make a blog a super-search star.
  - Use the URLs of the top ranked pages in a tool like ahrefs or MOZ to find the inbound links to the page. You know the bloggers that linked to the page are interested in your topic and may be interested in your new content. Have a VA look through each of these links to get contact details of the blogger.
  - It used to be as easy as reaching out to each of these sites in an email with something like, "Hey, I noticed you linked to this other post. Thought you might like this post I put together." That was before the technique became popular and everyone started using the same generic email for outreach.
  - Instead of a generic form letter, try getting on a few of the blogger's radar through social media first. Share a few of their posts and comment for a week or two. Then email them asking for their opinion on a new article you wrote, something you're really trying to turn into a great resource.
  - Ask a few bloggers for input to add in the post and add their link. When the post is published, they are more likely to share it around and may even link to it themselves.

Like most scalable link-building strategies, you're likely to get maybe 20% of your blogger emails answered and less than that will actually link to your post but that's all it will take to make a blog post jump in search. Just ten inbound links can really boost a post high enough to start getting natural links.

Infographics Still Work in Getting Blog Links

Infographics may not be as novel as they once were but still work well for getting links and making a blog visually persuasive to readers. People are visually-driven and they will share things that they find visually appealing.

Most people brainstorm an idea that they'd like to turn into an infographic on their blog. That's ok but it's not the best way to get huge blog traffic from your infographics.

Instead, start with one of your posts that is already getting good search traffic. Something that is ranking on the first page of Google or close to it for a bunch of keyword phrases. Remember, you find the keywords for which a post is ranking by using the Google Search Console → Search Analytics → Toggle the Pages button and then the Queries button.

Share your infographic on the sites mentioned in chapter six and include it in your post or in a new post. I try doing at least one infographic a month and sometimes two or three.

There are two other ways to promote your infographics for links back to your site.

- Offer to write a guest post of 500 – 700 words around the graphic for another blogger. You can reuse the same infographic for a few guest posts but write original content for each blog. It's a great way to stand out from simple text guest posts.

- If the infographic is really interesting, you can also just email out to your blogger contacts as a heads up. Most won't share your graphic or link to it but even a 5% response rate on 100 emails is five new links!

I've analyzed my infographic posts versus posts without infographics and those that include a graphic get an average of 2.6 times more links. That's huge for SEO.

Remember, it doesn't really take that much to boost a post with a semi-competitive keyword to the top of Google. Getting 20 or 30 good links through different link-building strategies and just the natural links that come from providing quality content will be enough.

Best of and Resource Page Backlinks

Bloggers often put together resource pages and 'best of' posts for their readers. Getting on these pages is one of the most scalable types of link-building you can do. It will take a couple hours to filter through potential targets but can yield dozens of links back to your post.

Your first step is to find resource pages and 'best of' posts on other blogs.

- Google searching including [keyword] plus "inURL:?" where ? is something like resources, links, or sites. This will give search for posts about the keyword and have one of those words (links, resources, sites) in the URL.
    - o Use this search in your Chrome browser with the MOZBar on so you can see the page and domain authority for each site.
    - o Scan and click through to the pages that look like they might be good link opportunities.
    - o Focus on those with a page authority over 15 and where they are linking to posts like the one you want to promote.

- Some other searches to try include:
  - ○ [keyword] + "useful links" or "helpful links"
  - ○ You can also use the "intitle:?" search with these words to find blog post titles with the word in the title, i.e. intitle:resources

This first step can take an hour or two but you can put together a list of hundreds of potential websites.

Your next step is to reach out to the sites and suggest your post. The great thing about resource pages and 'best of' posts is that they are specifically there to share great resources to readers. It's not like you are asking for a link on just any page, you're offering a great resource to their readers.

Be honest when emailing other bloggers. Just point out that you came across their resource page while reading the blog and thought that their readers might be interested in your resource.

If you spent your time making sure that the resource page is really relevant to the post you are trying to promote, you should have a good response rate from your emails. This means upwards of 5% or even higher in links…that's five inbound links to a post for every 100 emails you send. It doesn't seem like much but these are quality links that will really boost your search ranking.

Link Roundup Posts

Getting on link roundup posts is similar to getting on resource pages. These roundup posts are a little more common and you'll get on a lot of them just by being part of a blogger community on Facebook.

There are two ways to get links from roundup posts.

The first way is the most natural but harder to use strategically. If you are a member of blogger groups on Facebook, or any other social network, you will notice people regularly asking for input on a post they are writing.

These are extremely easy links to get. All you need is two or three sentences that answer the blogger's question and drop your link. Make sure the linked post is relevant to the question and there's a good chance they will link to it when they quote you in the post.

The second way to get on roundup posts is more strategic and involves searching for past posts and emailing the blogger. It's the same method as getting on resource pages but you change your search for words like 'roundup', 'weekly roundup', or 'best of the web'.

It helps if the blogger recognizes your name when your email reaches their inbox. You usually do this by regularly commenting on their blog or sharing their posts on Twitter but it might not be plausible if you're reaching out to hundreds of bloggers to get on roundup or resource page posts. It's part of the reason the response rate on these scalable link-building strategies is only about 5% but they still work to get a good amount of links.

Writing your own roundup posts is a great way to get backlinks from other bloggers and to get on their radar for more links on their websites. Reach out in blogger groups for responses to a specific question and ask people to link their best post. When you publish the post, make sure to email the bloggers included and ask them to share the post on social media.

Broken Link-Building

I avoided broken link-building for a long time. Big mistake!

The strategy can be one of your easiest and best link-building tools.

About 95% of bloggers give up and quit updating their site before six months of blogging. Even larger websites sometimes close-up.

If you link to one of those sites from your blog then when the site goes down that link will be 'broken'. A reader will see one of those annoying 404 Page Not Found pages if they click on it.

Besides a bad experience for your readers, Google hates broken links because it makes it look like you're not updating your website.

Broken link-building is about reaching out to bloggers that are linking to a 'broken' or non-existent page and suggesting another resource that might fit in its place.

The blogger gets a heads-up and can update their link with another great resource for their readers. You get a link to your page…it's a win, win.

Your first step is to prospect for broken links:

- Search for pages that point out to a lot of other pages. You can combine this method with the resource pages link-building strategy.

- You then want to extract all the linked URLs from each page. There are tools online like Domain Hunter Plus and Check My Links that will make this easier. These tools will also check each link to see if it is a broken or 404 page.

- Use the Wayback Machine at web.archive.org to make sure the broken page is similar to the page you want to promote. The Wayback Machine looks for old copies of the broken page on the internet so you can see what information it provided when it was live.

- Use another tool called a backlink checker to find all the links pointing to each relevant 404 page. Moz open site, ahrefs or the Majestic bulk backlink checker all do this. This is going to spit out a list of all the sites that are linking to that broken page.

- Click through to each linking site to make sure it is a good target for your link. The best link targets are non-commercial sites with at least 20 domain authority. You also want to make sure the link would be relevant, i.e. the resource you will be suggesting is relevant for the information they wanted to offer their readers.

- Find the contact information to websites you want to suggest your replacement link. You can do this individually by searching through their website or use any number of tools. I like Buzzstream but you can find other tools by searching Google for "Contact Finder"

- Email the website to heads up on the broken link and suggest your replacement.
  - Keep your outreach emails brief, no more than five or six sentences.
  - Establish your credibility in the first sentence, i.e. who are you?
  - Write as if you are a reader that happened upon the broken link rather than someone targeting their site.
  - The email should be casual, like one friend to another just pointing out a missing resource.
  - Try to use their name in the email if you found it in the contact search.

Broken Link-building Template Email:

Hey Karen,

I was searching for articles on [keyword] and came across your post [link page with broken link].

I clicked through the link to [link broken link] and got a 404 error message. Looks like the page isn't working anymore.

I'm a [your credentials] and just put together a great resource that matches the broken linked page. I'm really happy how the article came out and put a ton of work into making it as detailed as possible. It's here [link your resource] if you want to check it out.

....

I've heard of people offering a few links as the replacement link, giving the website a choice of which they use. I've also heard some people not suggesting a new link but telling the blogger they have a great resource and then sending the link suggestion in a follow-up email if the blogger asks for it.

Broken link-building takes time but gets a better response rate than some of the other techniques. You can expect upwards of 10% response or better which can mean dozens of links if you put the time in. The strategy is scalable, meaning you'll find a lot of potential link targets fast so it's definitely one you want to put in your SEO process.

Scholarship Pages and Huge EDU Links

We're taking a break from page-specific SEO for a minute because I want to share one of my favorite ways to get some great links and really boost all the pages on your blog.

You should never buy links or you risk facing Google's wrath and getting penalized but there is one powerful way to get links by giving money away. Understand that Google loves .edu and .gov inbound links. The educational and government sites aren't just going to link to anyone so a lot of inbound links to your site makes your blog look like a trusted source.

One of the easiest ways to get a lot of .edu links to your blog is through offering a scholarship. Many colleges have pages on their websites linking to scholarship and financial aid opportunities for their students. Before you write off an annual scholarship of $500 or $1,000 as too expensive, how much would 50+ .edu backlinks and dozens of guest posts be worth?

- Put together a scholarship page and put it in your footer menu. You can model it off my personal finance scholarship on PeerFinance101. Be sure to include the amount, eligibility requirements, deadlines, contact details and what's required of students. Treat the page as any other an optimize for a keyword or two, writing at least 500 words.

- Search on Google for 'Outside Scholarship Opportunities' to find a few college scholarship pages. Copy the link to five or ten of the scholarships on the page that are from commercial websites or blogs. Through a tool like ahrefs or MOZ, you can find all the .edu pages that link to these scholarship pages.

- You can also do a Google search for different terms like 'scholarship page' or 'third-party scholarships' for .edu pages that might link to your scholarship page. You're going to want to build a huge list of colleges, at least a couple hundred. Have a virtual assistant go to each of these pages and find the contact information for the administrator.

- Reach out for inclusion on the school's scholarship page. You can expect around 10% of the pages will link back to yours. Building up 50 or so .edu links has the potential to really make a blog rock higher in search. Requiring that participants submit an essay is also a great way to get content for your blog.

Other Oft-Missed Backlink Strategies

I use the skyscraper approach and resource page links on the most important pages I want to rank but there are also a lot of miscellaneous link-building strategies that I will use every now and then.

Most of these strategies take a little longer and are not as scalable but can still be a great source for a dozen or so links to a page.

You'll get a feel for each strategy and which you prefer pretty quickly. Keep a couple on your list for use regularly but don't feel like you need to work all of them all the time.

Testimonials

Commercial websites are always looking for testimonials from customers and will often link back to the user's website.

Make a list of all the products you use on a regular basis and visit the company's website. They may already have a testimonials page or some scattered throughout the site. Find a contact email and offer your own testimonial and link back to your site.

Blog Commenting

Commenting on other blogger's posts isn't quite as popular as it used to be but it's still an important part of the complete SEO process.

Blog commenting isn't necessarily for the link you get when commenting. These are nofollow links that mean little to Google so they won't boost your ranking in search. Some SEO specialists say that even these nofollow links help to improve a post's link profile, the fact that blogs in your industry are linking to your site is a good signal.

The real goal of blog commenting is just as an outreach tool. Bloggers see you are regularly following their site and may do the same for your blog. They are much more likely to reply to your requests for guest posts or other link-building strategies. They are also more likely to link to your content naturally if they see something they like.

There are freelancers online, mostly from foreign countries, that will do your blog commenting for you...Don't do This! These are all the crap comments you see and automatically delete from your blog.

Genuinely read through other blogs and leave a legit comment. You can scan a post in less than a minute and leave a two- or three-sentence comment relevant to the article. Scheduling 30 minutes each day to visit other blogs and comment can put you on dozens of bloggers' radar.

Podcast Interviews

Podcasts are the new way to blog and podcast interviews are the new-age equivalent to guest posting…except easier.

The process works a lot like guest posting. You can research podcasts related to your blog on the Apple iTunes store.

As with most link-building, it helps to develop a relationship before reaching out for an interview. This means following the podcaster, leaving a review and sharing their content on social media.

When you do land an interview, make sure you have listened to a couple of episodes so you know what questions to expect. Podcasters listen to other podcasts so giving a great interview is your best way to get other interviews.

Besides being ready with your answers before the interview, make sure you are in a quiet place where you won't be bothered during the interview. A great way to reinvest in your business is by spending on a quality microphone and webcam that can produce the quality audio/video that will impress others.

Podcasters will usually give you a couple of links on their show notes page. Don't throw it away by offering a homepage link. Ask them if you can link to a specific page that relates to what you talked about in your interview.

Link-building is one of the most neglected aspects of blogging. Because of that, it's also one of the best ways to get out ahead and get your pages ranked on Google. Some of the strategies will take a little time but it's worth every second. What good is it to spend hours or days writing a post if no one is going to see it? Spend a few of those hours getting links back to the post and get it on that first page of Google.

The Republishing Secret that Triples Traffic

I've always said there's no secret to making money blogging. All the best bloggers I know make money because they write consistently for years and slowly build huge blog traffic through search and a following.

There is one trick I've learned though that can be a huge boost to your monthly visitors. It can improve some of your best posts and can boost you to the first page on Google.

In fact, I started using this blogging secret in July of 2015 and have seen average traffic to each post surge by 246% just on this one method.

It's the last step in my SEO process and is a great way to get everything you can out of every post.

It's called republishing and I almost don't want to let the secret out. Ok, it feels like a secret but there's actually a lot of bloggers doing it…just not doing it correctly.

I'll cover why republishing works so well in boosting blog traffic and then the process I use to get more visitors and make more money blogging.

What is Blog Post Republishing?

Once you've published an article on your blog, you can do one of two things with it if you want to make changes. Making your changes in WordPress and clicking Update will change the post but will keep the previous publication date and the post will be archived somewhere in the basement of your blog.

Your other option is to republish the blog post as a new article by clicking Edit and changing the date to current.

You actually want to change the date to a few minutes into the future before you hit publish but we'll get into why pretty soon. One more quick warning, don't change the permalink URL to the post when you republish!

When you republish a post, it becomes a new post on your site. The date changes and it rockets to the front of your blogroll for everyone to see. Since the majority of blog traffic is new visitors and most find your site through search, it's likely a new post for anyone but your most die-hard readers.

I kept track of traffic to my republished posts through Google Analytics over the first year of republishing. I still track which posts have been republished but have stopped noting the change in traffic...well because it's such a huge boost in blog visitors that it could be half as effective and I'd still do it.

When you track traffic to your republished posts, you'll want to record 30-day views before republishing and then 30-day views after waiting a month. Don't track views for the immediate 30 days following because those include a lot of direct and social traffic rather than mostly search visitors. Of the 20 posts I republished to two blogs, only three saw traffic declines while a few saw traffic increases of 500% or more.

The average increase was 247% meaning that a post that got 100 visitors before republishing was getting 347 visitors afterwards. One post went from 67 views to 1,284 views after republishing!

		A		B	C	D	30-Day Organic Search Views Before	30-Day Organic Search Views After (Following 30-Day Waiting Period)	Percent Change in Organic Search Views
	Blog Post Title		Blog Post URL		Original Publish Date	Date of Post Update			
The Ultimate List of Peer to Peer Or			http://peerfinance101.com/make-r		3/16/2015	11/2/2015	67	1284	1816.4%
top 5 crowdfunding platforms for equity investing					11/19/2014	9/28/2015	38	360	847.4%
How the Rich Stay Rich					Nov-14	████████	15	111	640.0%
Forget Crowdfunding, Get a Peer Loan Instead					1/1/2015	10/6/2015	9	59	555.6%
Investment Risks in Peer Lending			http://peerfinance101.com/avoid-3		11/25/2014	9/17/2015	7	39	457.1%
Borrower Risks in Peer Lending			http://peerfinance101.com/avoid-3		12/3/2014	9/3/2015	15	80	433.3%
Bad Credit and Credit Score Factors			http://peerfinance101.com/dealing		11/14/2014	9/10/2015	8	29	262.5%
How to Make Money Online Selling			http://peerfinance101.com/make-r		3/30/2015	8/20/2015	194	672	246.4%

There are a couple of reasons why republishing posts works so well.

Google has a recency factor in its search algorithm. We don't know how strong it is but newer posts are favored over older content. Of course older content usually has more links so will do better but their search power will start to fade after a while.

Republishing posts makes them look new to Google but they still have all the inbound links and search equity of the older post.

Within the republishing process, you're going to be going back through the post to update and improve it. Think about how much you've learned blogging and how much you could improve some of your earlier content. This means more content, better on-page SEO and a better reader experience.

All of these contribute to a stronger search ranking for your post.

Republishing also gives you a chance to increase the frequency of your content, another factor in Google's search algorithm. A blog that updates frequently with new content is going to be crawled more by those beautiful Google spiders.

How to Republish a Blog Post

There's no formalized process for republishing blog posts but there are some things you can do to get a better Google boost and to make more money off your best blog posts. I know bloggers that basically just change the date on their post and republish, missing out on a huge opportunity for higher traffic and more money.

It's best to start with posts at least six months old and ones that are already getting a decent amount of visitors.

Check your Google Analytics under Behavior – Site Content – All Pages to find your most popular blog posts. If you get a lot of blog traffic from Pinterest or another source other than Google, these might not be your best search-ranked posts but it's a good place to start.

You can also look to your Google Webmaster tool to find your best posts for Google search traffic. We hit on this earlier in the book.

- Go to the Search Analytics section of your Google Search Console (Webmaster Tools)
- Click the circle next to 'Pages' to show the pages that get the most clicks and impressions on Google
- You can click on a specific page and then on 'Queries' to see the keywords the page is ranking for as well as the average position in search.

This is important because you're going to go back through the post to keyword optimize it. This means making the post stand out in Google's eyes as really authoritative content around a narrow subject.

Refer back to the chapter on On-Page SEO but here are a few points you'll want to remember when upgrading your post.

- Add H-tags with the keyword phrase to a post headline and several section headings

- Are there any places in the content where you can fit the keyword or a synonym?

- Add new content around the topic, using the keyword phrase where appropriate

- Link any other posts from your blog that are relevant and provide more info to readers

- Add any appropriate images and make sure you use the keyword in the filename and meta-tags

If you've got the Yoast SEO plugin, you'll be able to track some of your on-page SEO improvements.

You also want to read through the post and do any general updating and editing. You'll be amazed...and maybe a little embarrassed at some of the mistakes you made on your first posts. Republishing gives you a chance to keep new readers from getting turned off on your blog from grammar mistakes and wonky sentences.

The best part of republishing posts, beyond the huge boost to blog traffic, is the opportunity to go back through and monetize your most popular content. Ever heard of the 80/20 rule? Well in blogging it's more like 10% of your posts account for 90% of your blog traffic each month.

My top ten posts account for 67% of monthly traffic, you better believe I'm trying to make money off those ten articles.

When you republish a post, add any affiliate links where appropriate. Don't force it but there's usually at least one affiliate that you can fit into the conversation by adding a paragraph or two. If you don't use affiliate links much, add a callout and link to another product or book.

Besides your best performing posts, try going back to republish your review posts of affiliates or other posts that are already making money. It's just as easy to make more money from a post that's already converting than it is to figure out how to make money off a non-monetized post.

When you're done optimizing and updating the post, click Edit and change the publication date for a few minutes into the future.

You don't want to schedule it any more than a few minutes into the future because the URL will be inactive until it publishes. That means all the inbound links will be broken and webmasters might decide to unlink the post. Scheduling for a couple of minutes into the future gives WordPress enough time to schedule it but the inbound links won't be broken long enough for anyone to notice.

Treat the republished post just as you would any other new content. Share it out on social media and promote it to readers to get those social signals alerting Google that there's a new post on the blog.

A few more things to remember when republishing posts:

- Don't forget: DO NOT change the Permalink URL address! This is where all your inbound links and your search power points. Changing the post URL will break these links and you'll lose your search ranking.

- Republishing won't work if you have the date in your Permalink URL address. You'll need to change your permalink structure on the blog first, redirecting all your old URLs to the new permalink structure.

- Content is king so don't be afraid to add to your posts. You're saving a lot of time by not having to write an entirely new post, spend a little of that time in making your republished post exceptional.

Republishing is a great wrap-up to your SEO process on a page. By the time the post is six months old, you will have built up a strong profile of links and will have given Google time to rank the page. Republishing it gives it an extra boost and can really bump it higher to get a few more natural backlinks and a ton of traffic.

Wrapping up Your SEO Strategy

SEO doesn't have to take up all your time but you can't afford to ignore it as a blogger. One of the best ways to be successful is to watch for things your competition is avoiding and then use the information to jump ahead.

Few bloggers do much for SEO and even fewer have a process they use regularly to rank their pages. They might build in some ideas into their on-page writing but almost nobody I know actually puts off-page SEO concepts like link-building and link-sharing on their weekly calendar.

That means just a little effort on your part can rank even the smallest blogs on the first page of Google for massive traffic.

Plan one day a week to work on SEO, whether it's keyword research for upcoming posts or repurposing content into other formats or link-building. It may seem like a lot but it needs to be on your schedule or it risks getting pushed back when you're 'too busy'.

How to Use the SEO Strategies in this Book

I've got a confession to make. Even I don't use the entire SEO strategy for every single post I publish.

I've got six blogs and try to publish at least once a week to each. Sometimes I just want to write a quick post about a topic, something that regular readers will enjoy.

Sometimes I just don't have the time to write a 3,000+ word post for each blog and then do all the linking and outreach.

That's fine and you shouldn't feel like every post has to reach #1 on Google. There are some parts of the process that you'll want to use on ever post you publish while you might save others for the really great posts that have the potential to bring in mountains of traffic and sales.

Parts of the process you should do with every post:

- **Keyword research**: This really takes less than 20 minutes and can mean a huge difference in eventually ranking your post. Put together a list of at least 5-10 keywords for the post and check out the monthly volume and competitiveness in search. It's better to rank well for a smaller volume keyword than not at all for a high-volume keyword.

- **On-page SEO** will become a natural part of your writing. You'll always want to include keywords and related words at strategic parts of the post as well as naming images. It takes just a few minutes to check your post after its written and work through a quick on-page checklist.

- **Internal linking and the Hub-and-Spoke strategy**: This is another easy part of your on-page SEO that doesn't take much time but leads to big gains. By internally linking your posts, you're not only giving them an SEO boost but also making it easy for readers to stay on your site.

- **Some link-building strategies**: I have built a huge resource list of blogs over the years that I will reach out to when I publish a new post. For most of my new posts, I run a quick check on ahrefs or MOZ for related resource pages, roundups and 'best of' posts to email for inclusion. These are the best, scalable link-building strategies that take less time than some of the others but can get a couple of really good links.

- **Blog commenting**: Commenting on a couple of other blogs each day is a great way to keep in touch with other bloggers and get some traffic coming back to your site. Following a few other blogs will give you ideas on what to write about and help improve your own writing.

You'll find that some posts shoot to the top of Google without much help anyway. For one reason or another, these posts pick up a lot of natural links and get ranked in search. For these and for the posts you really want to rank from the beginning, you can carry through with the rest of the SEO strategy.

- **Repurposing your posts with other media**: This can actually be fairly quick and easy, especially if you train an assistant to help. It's also a great way to build your YouTube profile and start getting traffic from one of the biggest sites on the net. If I didn't boost the post originally with a few formats, I'll always make up an audio or video to share when republishing.

- **Guest posting**: Writing a quality guest post will take a couple of hours minimum so I usually reserve it only for really important posts. When I have a post with the potential to really bring in traffic and money, I'll write a few guest posts and get a link in each. It takes time but these links are gold for Google search. Try writing at least a couple of guest posts each month.

- **Link-building Strategies**: You can pick and choose the link-building strategies you do for each post and those you only do on some but you need to do at least a little link-building on everything you write. I reserve some of the more time-intensive strategies like infographics, broken link-building and interviews for my really important posts.

- **Republishing**: I republish posts regularly, usually once a week, but don't get to all the posts on the blog. You don't necessarily want to republish all the posts on your site either. You want some content with later dates to tell Google your blog is a time-tested resource for readers. It's a great strategy to use on your important posts once a year.

Note: There are people that would argue with me on this one, saying that you should put time to the complete SEO process for every single blog post even if it means posting much less frequently. They would argue that if you aren't committed to ranking #1 for every post then maybe it wasn't worth writing in the first place.

They've got a point and it wouldn't hurt to do everything you can to boost everything you publish. I've been successful just doing the full process on about half my posts but it's up to you how much further you want to take it.

Finally, don't forget that good SEO strategies and what you need to do to rank on Google are continuously changing.

Google changes its program to devalue a particular source of links or to place higher value on others. Bloggers overuse one strategy, everyone gets tired of it and it becomes less effective.

This doesn't mean you'll have to totally revamp your SEO process every year. Just follow some of the SEO blogs in the resources section. You'll pick up on new ideas constantly and clue in to any major changes implemented by Google.

A Special Request

I hope you've enjoyed **Google SEO** and found the advice to be helpful in revealing the process to get your posts ranked on Google. This process has helped me rank for more than 1,700 keywords on the first page of Google and I know it will work for you to bring massive search traffic.

I'd like to ask one favor as you finish reading the book. Reader reviews are extremely important to the success of a book on Amazon. Reviews play a big part in determining the rank of a book and how many people see it when searching.

If you found the book to be helpful, would you please leave a review on the Amazon page?

It's really easy to do and does not have to be a long, detailed review.

Please click here to leave a review on Amazon

- Just go to the book's page on Amazon (or through the link above) and click on "customer reviews" or scroll down and click on "Write a customer review"
- Your review can be as short as a sentence or as long as you like. Just try describing what you liked about the book and any particular points from a chapter.

I always appreciate honest reviews.
Thank you so much!

Resources

I've mentioned a lot of SEO and other blogging resources in the book but wanted to highlight some of the best here in the last chapter.

You may not need all of these resources but check each out to see which fit with your overall blogging strategy. Some are free while others may charge a monthly fee.

Other Books on Blogging and Passive Income

What good is tons of Google search traffic if you're not making any money off it? I don't know about you but I'm in this blogging thing to make money…lots of it!

That's why I'm pairing this Google SEO book with a simultaneous launch of Make Money Blogging and the nine best ways bloggers make money. You'll find a detailed guide into each of the nine money-making methods including how to get started and how much you can expect to make.

The book is laid out to get the easy money first with PPC advertising and other sources of quick blogging cash. It then helps you move into the bigger money-makers like self-publishing, affiliates and making five-figures a month with webinars.

If you aren't using these nine methods, you aren't making as much money as you could on your blog!

Click to Get Make Money Blogging on Amazon or Audible.

Cut through the B.S. of passive income myths for the real strategies to make money in four popular passive income businesses.

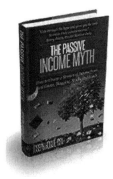 I give you the real scoop on how to make money in real estate, blogging, stocks and bonds and rank each by their passive income potential.

No 3am infomercial hype here, just a detailed process into different strategies to make money every month whether you're working or not!

Get The Passive Income Myth on Amazon or Audible.

SEO Tools to Consider

I've talked about some SEO tools throughout the book like ahrefs and MOZ. Some of them can get expensive but you can get a lot of data and insight from just a free trial. If nothing else, you might want to schedule a month each year for a big SEO push and subscribe to one of the tools for that month to get all your data.

Ahrefs is specifically geared to backlinks, keywords and other SEO data. Tons of info including competitor research and keyword tracking.

Buzzstream is a great tool for blogger outreach. You can search for bloggers in a specific niche and use the site's tools to send outreach and link-building campaigns.

Content Marketer is another outreach tool that helps find blogger email addresses and send outreach campaigns.

Yoast SEO plugin is the best WordPress plugin and a must for your site. Makes on-page SEO easy with the box at the bottom of your page editor.

Screaming Frog is one of the most popular tools for auditing your website, finding pages that need an SEO boost and ways to fix your blog for better ranking. It's got some great features in the free version.

MOZ Open Site Explorer(https://moz.com/researchtools/ose/) is another excellent tool and similar to Ahrefs for competitor research, linking opportunities and tracking.

SEO Blogs to Follow

Most of these blogs are operated by companies or people that offer SEO tools and services so the posts are naturally going to include how to use their tools. You won't find an aha-moment in ever post but you'll get some great ways to keep up with SEO and boost your pages.

My Work from Home Money, just one last shameless plug for my blog. You'll not only find great ideas on SEO and making money blogging but other ways to make money online and reach financial independence.

MOZ blog is geared to the SEO professional, someone that provides SEO services to other websites, so some of the posts can get a little technical. It's still one of my favorite resources for cutting-edge SEO techniques and some of the best research you'll find.

Backlinko is Brian Dean's blog on link-building and an excellent resource for blogger SEO. Brian doesn't update the blog often but when he does, he posts super-detailed content with lots of ideas.

Ahrefs Blog is another blog I follow regularly for blogger SEO. The ideas tend to require using the ahrefs tools but usually offer a few work-arounds and it's one of the best basic SEO sites available.

SearchEngineLand is another site mostly geared to the SEO professional but that's where you are really going to find the newest and best strategies. The site is a little harder to get around because everything is separated into categories but still worth a look every once in a while.

Google's official Webmaster blog is…yet another site for SEO geeks but it's the very first news on changes Google is going to be making.